ANDREW W.K.
THE VERY BEST 2001-2009

T0085452

Published by
Wise Publications
14-15 Berners Street, London W1T 3LJ, UK.

Exclusive Distributors:
Music Sales Limited
Distribution Centre, Newmarket Road, Bury St Edmunds, Suffolk IP33 3YB, UK.
Music Sales Pty Limited
20 Resolution Drive, Caringbah, NSW 2229, Australia.

Order No. AM998041 ISBN 978-1-84938-150-5

Photographs courtesy of: Jonathan Bachman, p2 (centre); p4 (background). Rick Day, front cover; p5 (top); p112 (background).
Douglas Dollars, p1; pp4 & 5 (background). Roe Ethridge, p5 (bottom). Jason Fisher, back cover.
Kentaro Kambe, p112 (top). Victoria Stevens, p2 (bottom). Andrew Strasser, p2 (top); p5 (centre); p112 (bottom).

Music arranged by Martin Shellard.
Music edited by Adrian Hopkins.
Music processed by Paul Ewers Music Design.
Designed by Tim Field.
Printed in the EU.
www.musicsales.com

WISE PUBLICATIONS
part of The Music Sales Group
London /New York /Paris /Sydney /Copenhagen /Berlin /Tokyo /Madrid

GUITAR TABLATURE EXPLAINED

Guitar music can be notated in three different ways: on a musical stave, in tablature, and in rhythm slashes.

RHYTHM SLASHES: are written above the stave. Strum chords in the rhythm indicated. Round noteheads indicate single notes.

THE MUSICAL STAVE: shows pitches and rhythms and is divided by lines into bars. Pitches are named after the first seven letters of the alphabet.

TABLATURE: graphically represents the guitar fingerboard. Each horizontal line represents a string, and each number represents a fret.

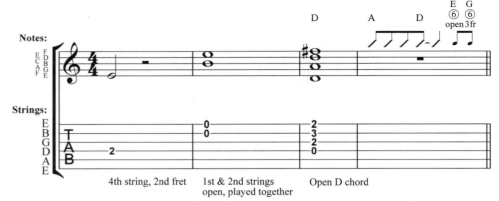

4th string, 2nd fret   1st & 2nd strings open, played together   Open D chord

Definitions for special guitar notation

SEMI-TONE BEND: Strike the note and bend up a semi-tone (½ step).

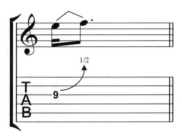

WHOLE-TONE BEND: Strike the note and bend up a whole-tone (full step).

GRACE NOTE BEND: Strike the note and bend as indicated. Play the first note as quickly as possible.

QUARTER-TONE BEND: Strike the note and bend up a ¼ step

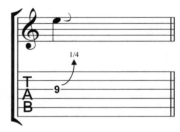

BEND & RELEASE: Strike the note and bend up as indicated, then release back to the original note.

COMPOUND BEND & RELEASE: Strike the note and bend up and down in the rhythm indicated.

PRE-BEND: Bend the note as indicated, then strike it.

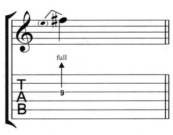

PRE-BEND & RELEASE: Bend the note as indicated. Strike it and release the note back to the original pitch.

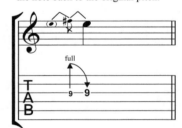

HAMMER-ON: Strike the first note with one finger, then sound the second note (on the same string) with another finger by fretting it without picking.

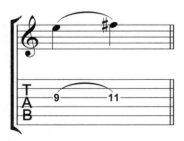

PULL-OFF: Place both fingers on the note to be sounded, strike the first note and without picking, pull the finger off to sound the second note.

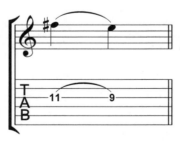

LEGATO SLIDE (GLISS): Strike the first note and then slide the same fret-hand finger up or down to the second note. The second note is not struck.

MUFFLED STRINGS: A percussive sound is produced by laying the first hand across the string(s) without depressing, and striking them with the pick hand.

NATURAL HARMONIC: Strike the note while the fret-hand lightly touches the string directly over the fret indicated.

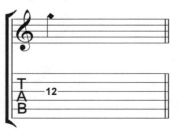

PICK SCRAPE: The edge of the pick is rubbed down (or up) the string, producing a scratchy sound.

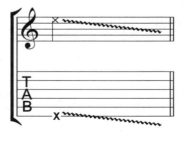

PALM MUTING: The note is partially muted by the pick hand lightly touching the string(s) just before the bridge.

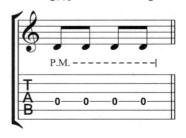

SHIFT SLIDE (GLISS & RESTRIKE) Same as legato slide, except the second note is struck.

6

TAP HARMONIC: The note is fretted normally and a harmonic is produced by tapping or slapping the fret indicated in brackets (which will be twelve frets higher than the fretted note.)

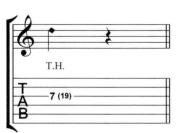

TAPPING: Hammer ('tap') the fret indicated with the pick-hand index or middle finger and pull-off to the note fretted by the fret hand.

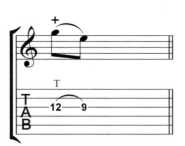

PINCH HARMONIC: The note is fretted normally and a harmonic is produced by adding the edge of the thumb or the tip of the index finger of the pick hand to the normal pick attack.

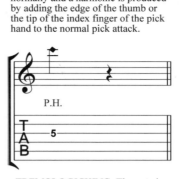

ARTIFICIAL HARMONIC: The note fretted normally and a harmonic is produced by gently resting the pick hand's index finger directly above the indicated fret (in brackets) while plucking the appropriate string.

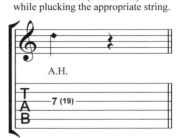

TRILL: Very rapidly alternate between the notes indicated by continuously hammering-on and pulling-off.

RAKE: Drag the pick across the strings with a single motion.

TREMOLO PICKING: The note is picked as rapidly and continously as possible.

ARPEGGIATE: Play the notes of the chord indicated by quickly rolling them from bottom to top.

SWEEP PICKING: Rhythmic downstroke and/or upstroke motion across the strings.

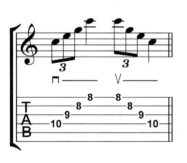

VIBRATO DIVE BAR AND RETURN: The pitch of the note or chord is dropped a specific number of steps (in rhythm) then returned to the original pitch.

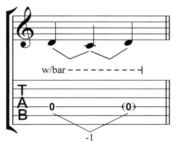

VIBRATO BAR SCOOP: Depress the bar just before striking the note, then quickly release the bar.

VIBRATO BAR DIP: Strike the note and then immediately drop a specific number of steps, then release back to the original pitch.

Additional musical definitions

  (accent)   Accentuate note (play it louder)

D.S. al Coda   Go back to the sign (𝄋), then play until the bar marked *To Coda* ⊕ then skip to the section marked ⊕ *Coda*

  (accent)   Accentuate note with greater intensity

D.C. al Fine   Go back to the beginning of the song and play until the bar marked *Fine.*

  (staccato)   Shorten time value of note

tacet   Instrument is silent (drops out).

⊓   Downstroke

V   Upstroke

   Repeat bars between signs

NOTE: Tablature numbers in brackets mean:
1. The note is sustained, but a new articulation (such as hammer-on or slide) begins
2. A note may be fretted but not necessarily played.

When a repeat section has different endings, play the first ending only the first time and the second ending only the second time.

7

YOU WILL REMEMBER TONIGHT

Words & Music by Andrew Wilkes-Krier

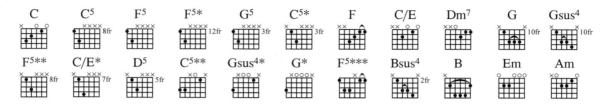

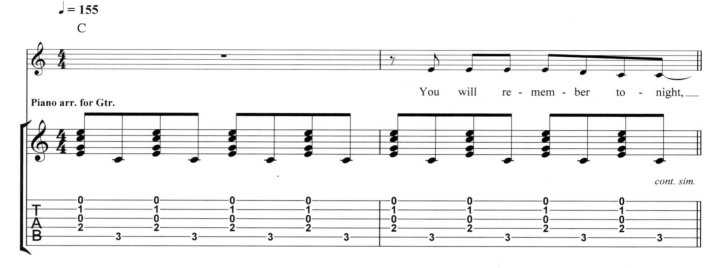

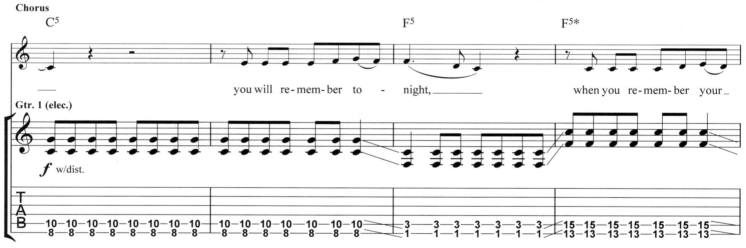

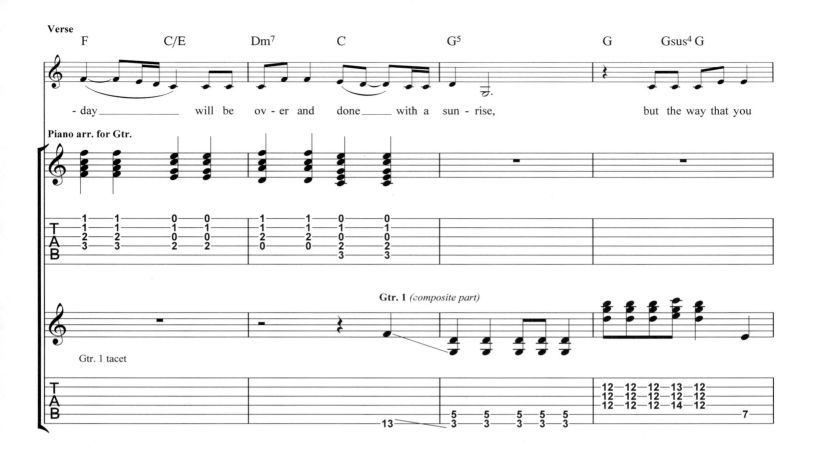

13

14

Guitar solo

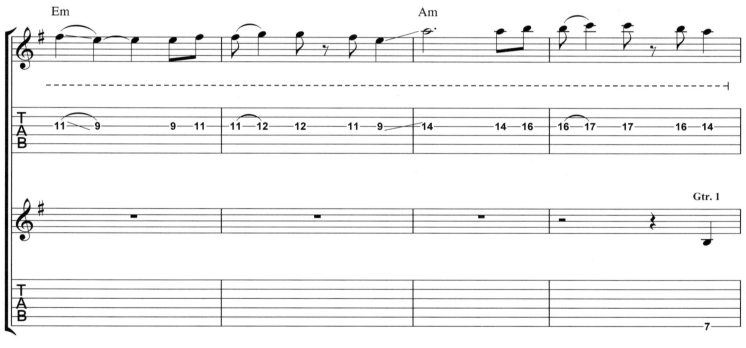

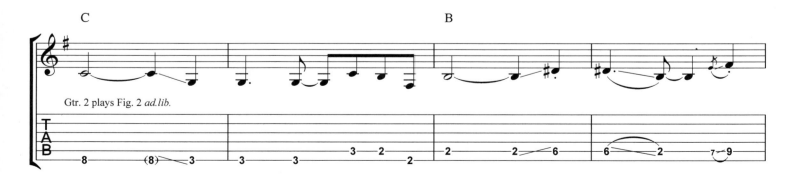

15

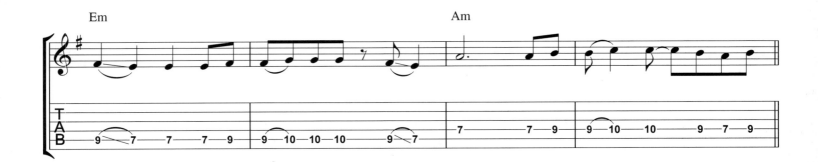

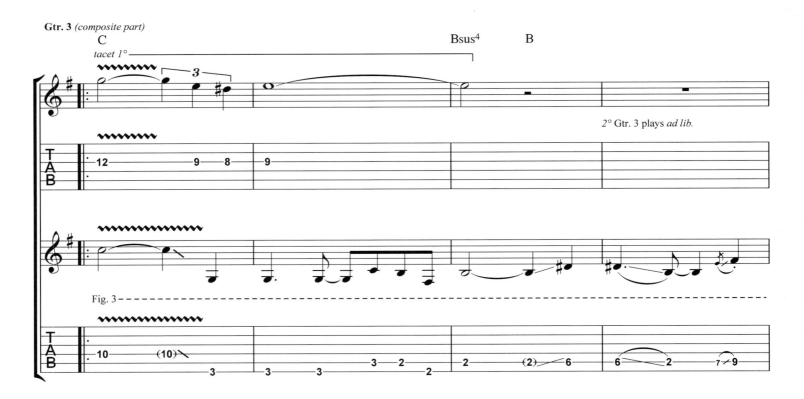

Gtr. 3 *(composite part)*

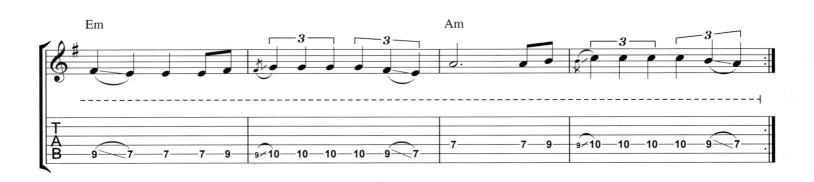

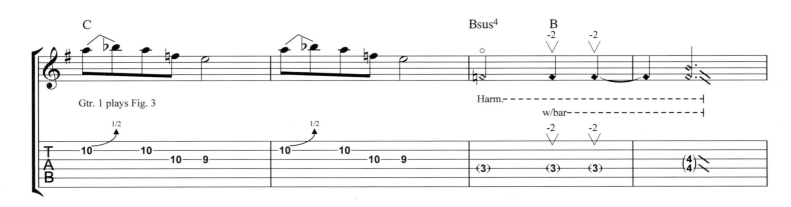

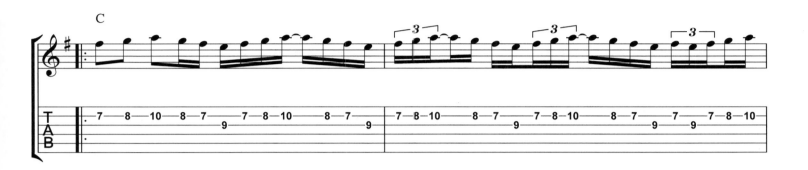

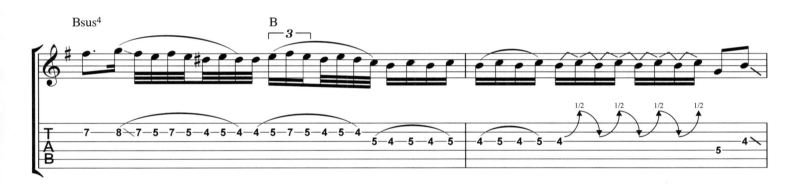

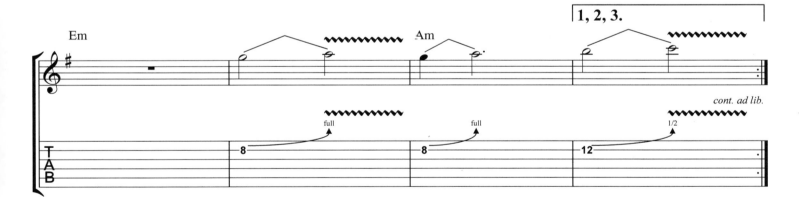

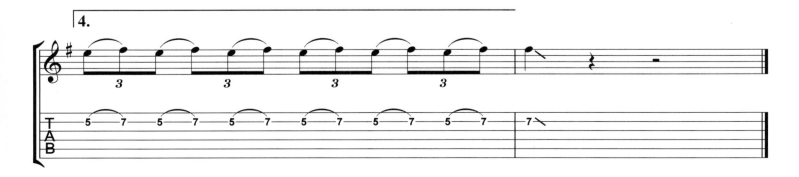

IT'S TIME TO PARTY

Words & Music by Andrew Wilkes-Krier

2. Touch - ing your mind   when it's tight in your hand,   now   dig it in deep,___ it's   time   to   par - ty.

Do - ing   it   fast,___ when you   do   it   a - lone,___ keep   cut - ting your   meat,___ it's   time   to   par - ty.

Pow - er   the   world,   plea-sure your - self,___   it's   not   too   late.___ it's   time   to   par - ty.

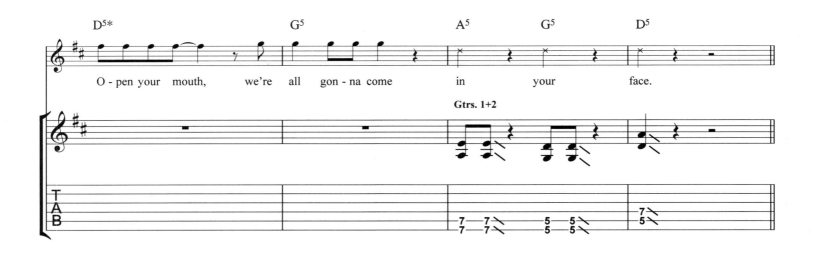

O - pen your   mouth,   we're   all   gon - na come   in   your   face.

Gtrs. 1+2

Interlude

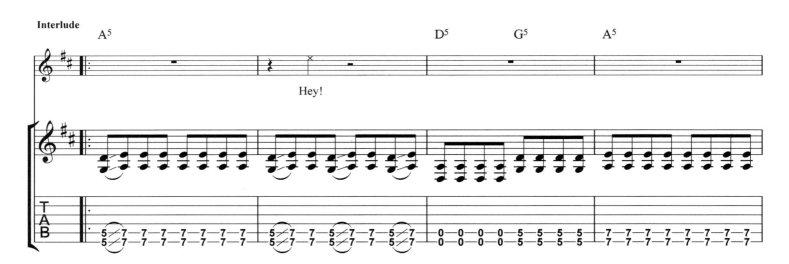

Hey!

20

21

WE WANT FUN

Words & Music by Andrew Wilkes-Krier

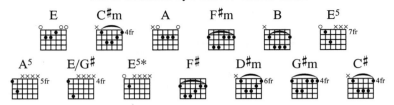

*chords implied by overall harmony

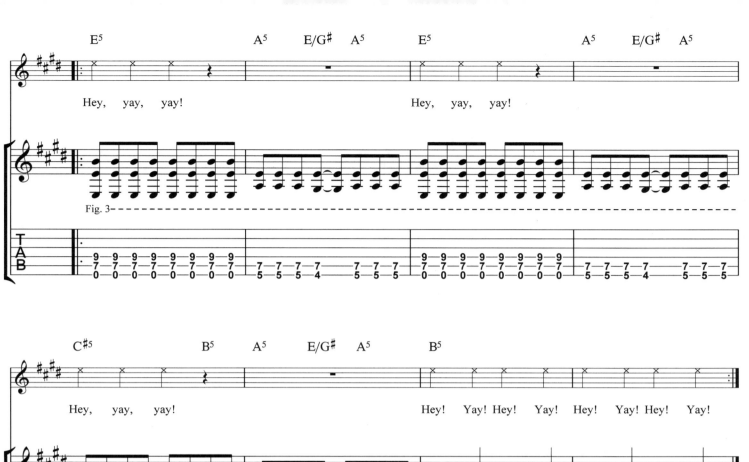

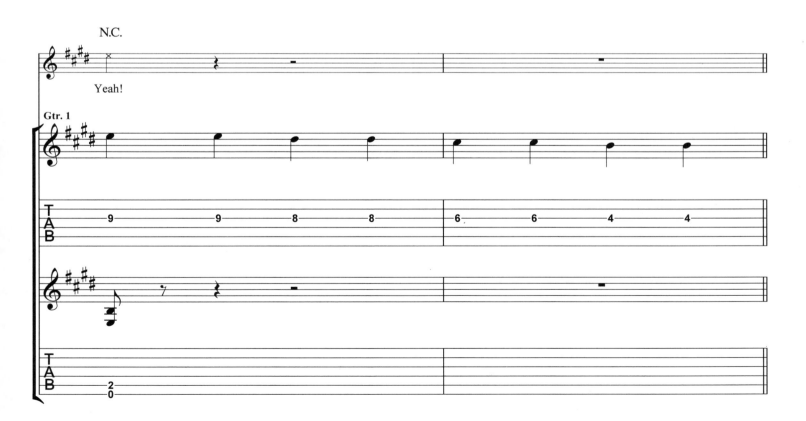

23

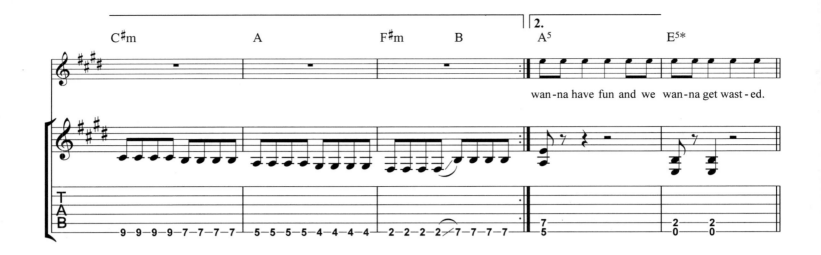

wan-na have fun and we wan-na get wast-ed.

Piano arr. for Gtr.

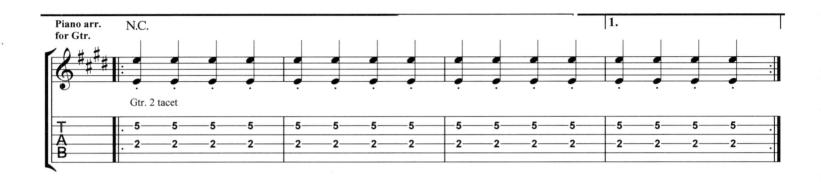

Gtr. 2 tacet

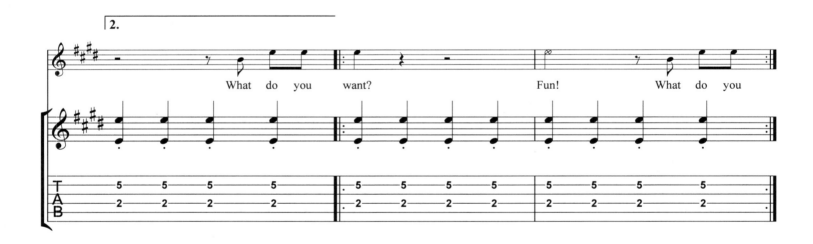

What do you want? Fun! What do you

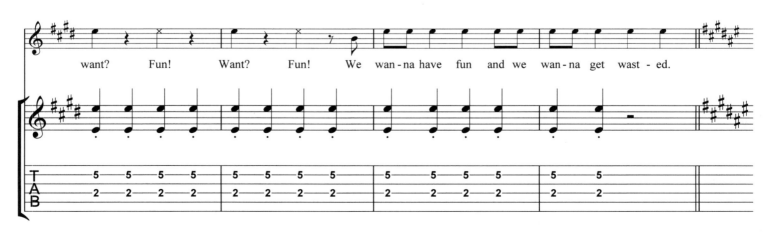

want? Fun! Want? Fun! We wan-na have fun and we wan-na get wast-ed.

TEAR IT UP

Words & Music by Andrew Wilkes-Krier

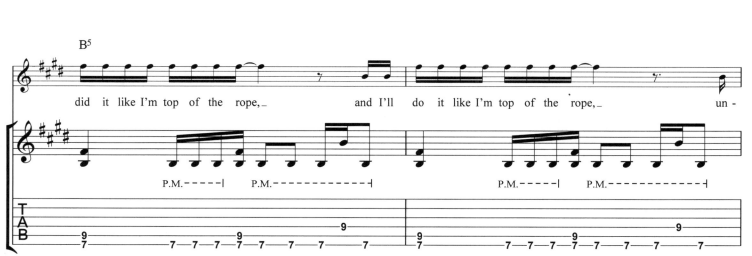

-til I let go,___ un-til I let go,___ I'll al-ways tear it up on my own.___ Tear it

Coda

(E)

Uh!

Gtr. 2

Gtr. 1

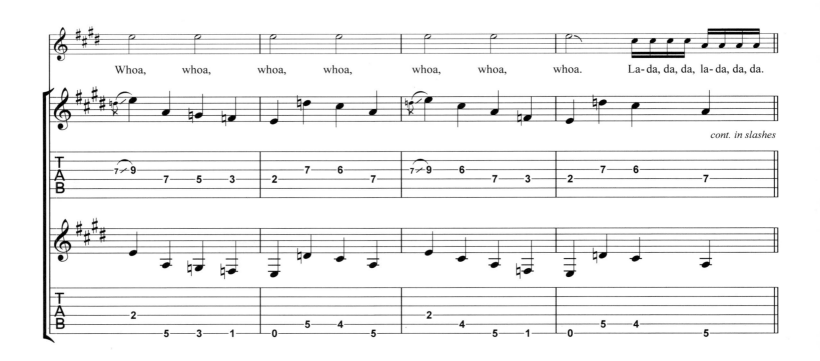

Whoa, whoa, whoa, whoa, whoa, whoa, whoa. La-da, da, da, la-da, da, da.

cont. in slashes

Chorus

up, tear it up, tear it up, tear it up, tear it up, tear it up all night.__ Tear it

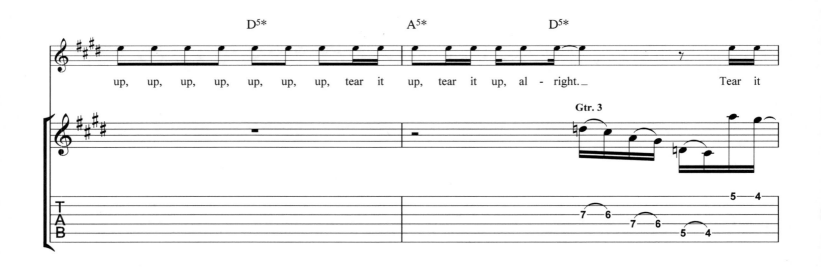

up, up, up, up, up, up, up, tear it up, tear it up, al - right.__ Tear it

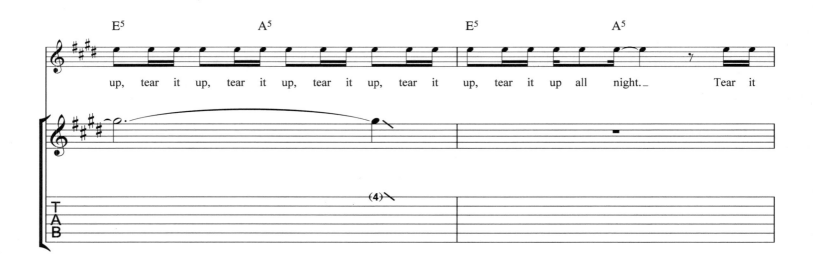

up, tear it up, tear it up, tear it up, tear it up, tear it up all night.__ Tear it

up, up, up, up, up, up, up, tear it up, tear it up, al - right.__ Tear it up.

Gtrs. 1+2+3 tacet

34

ONE BROTHER

Words & Music by Andrew Wilkes-Krier

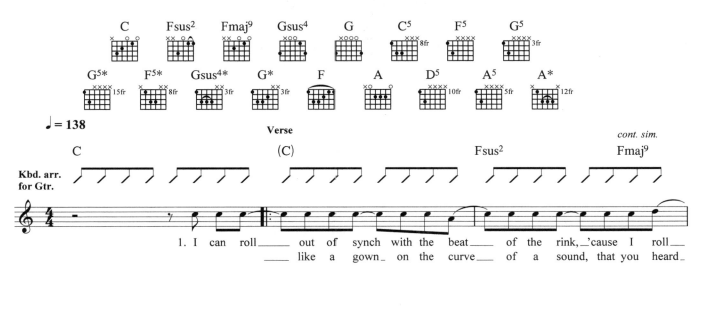

♩ = 138

Verse

cont. sim.

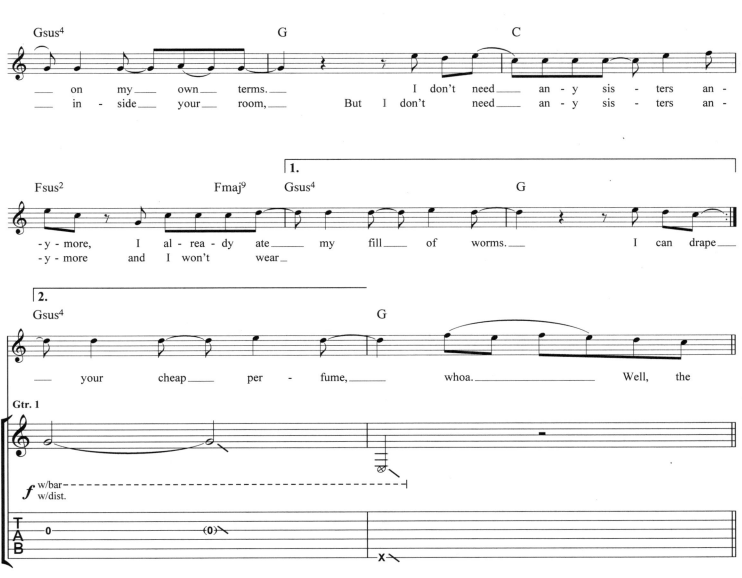

1. I can roll out of synch with the beat of the rink, 'cause I roll
   like a gown on the curve of a sound, that you heard

on my own terms. I don't need an-y sis-ters an-
in-side your room, But I don't need an-y sis-ters an-

1.
-y-more, I al-rea-dy ate my fill of worms. I can drape
-y-more and I won't wear

2.
your cheap per-fume, whoa. Well, the

Gtr. 1

f w/bar
w/dist.

𝄋
Chorus

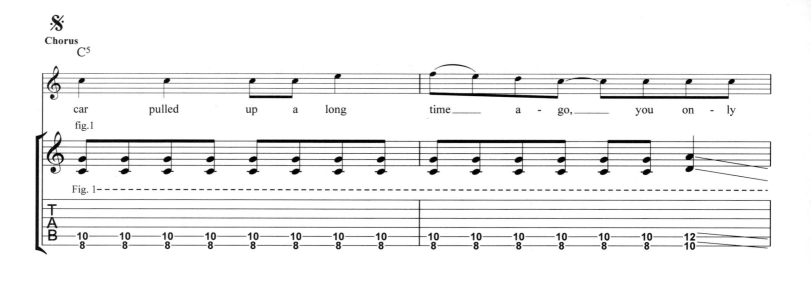

car   pulled   up   a   long   time___   a - go,___   you   on - ly

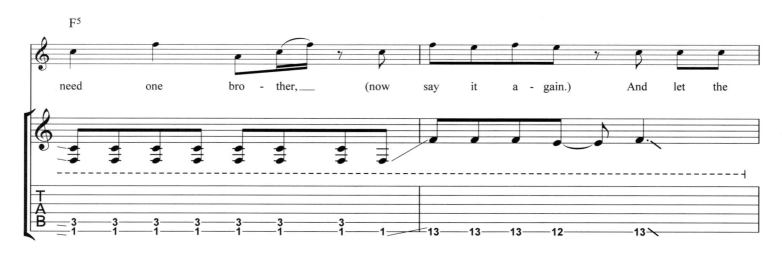

need   one   bro - ther,___   (now   say   it   a - gain.)   And   let   the

Gtr. 1 plays Fig. 1

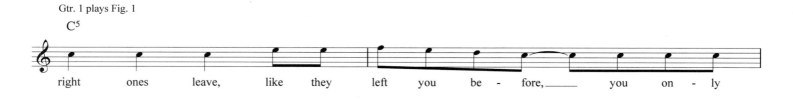

right   ones   leave,   like   they   left   you   be - fore,___   you   on - ly

got   one   bro - ther,___   (he's   on - ly   a   friend.)   And   you'll   be

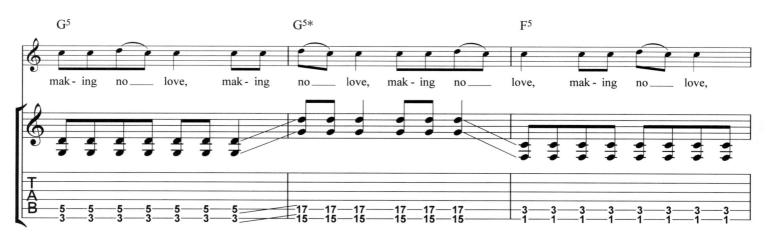

mak - ing   no___   love,   mak - ing   no___   love,   mak - ing   no___   love,   mak - ing   no___   love,

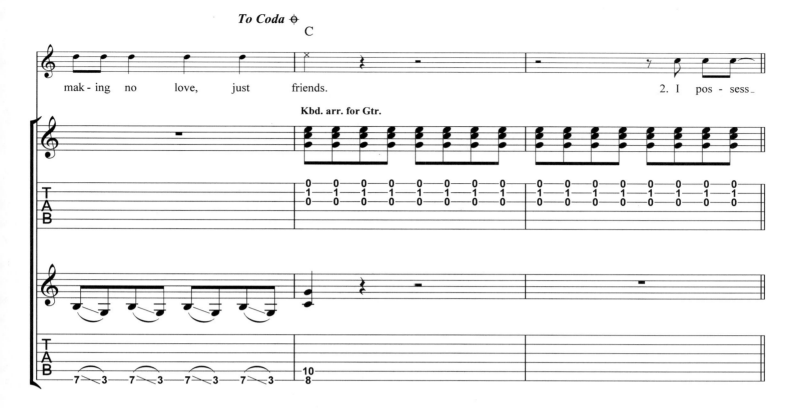

mak - ing no love, just friends.

2. I pos - sess

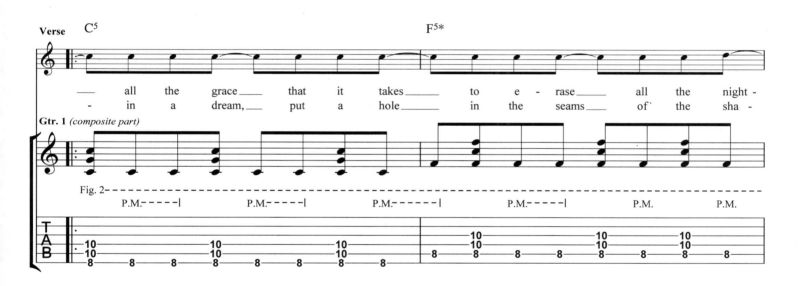

— all the grace___ that it takes___ to e - rase___ all the night -

- in a dream,___ put a hole_____ in the seams___ of' the sha -

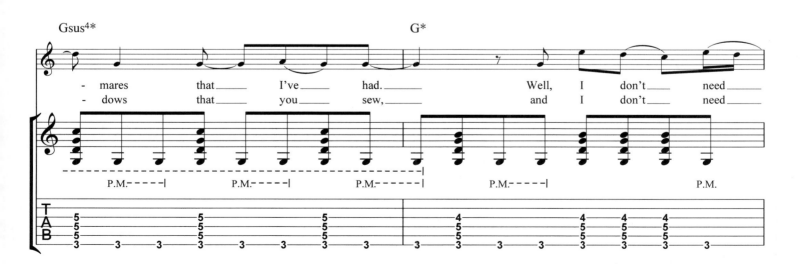

- mares that___ I've___ had._____ Well, I don't___ need_____

- dows that___ you___ sew,_____ and I don't___ need_____

38

VICTORY STRIKES AGAIN

Words & Music by Andrew Wilkes-Krier

*chords implied by overall harmony

41

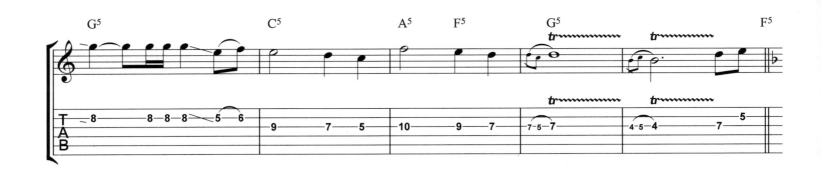

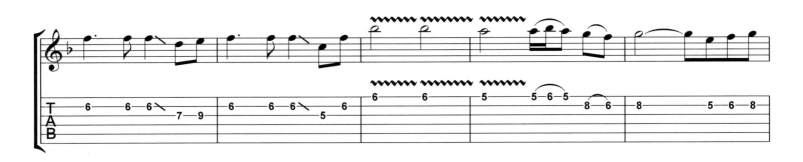

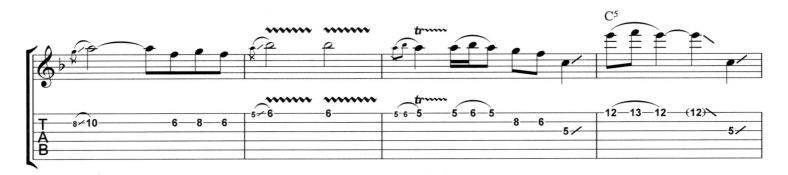

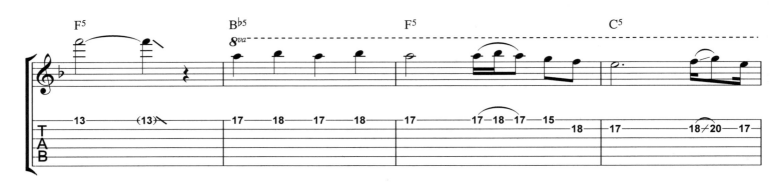

We all live like we are going to die.

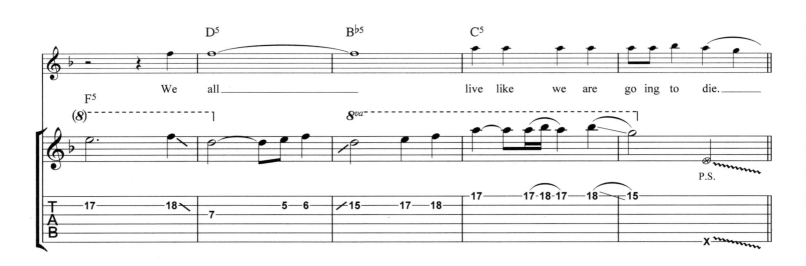

LONG LIVE THE PARTY

Words & Music by Andrew Wilkes-Krier

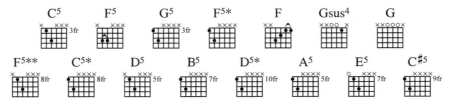

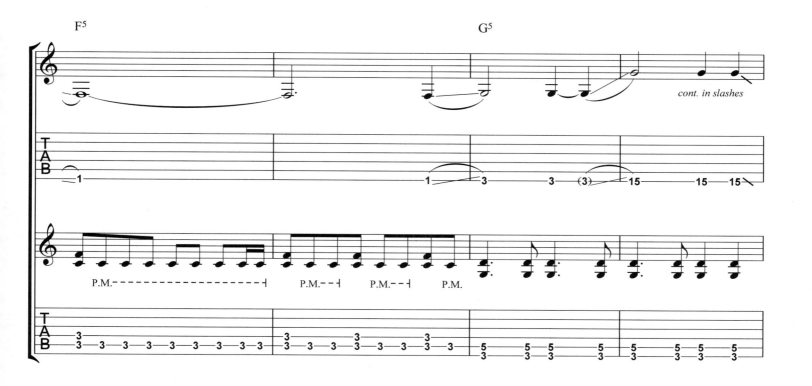

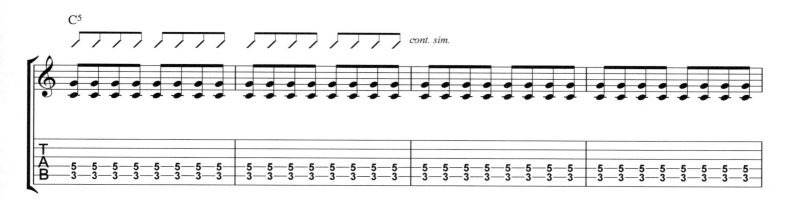

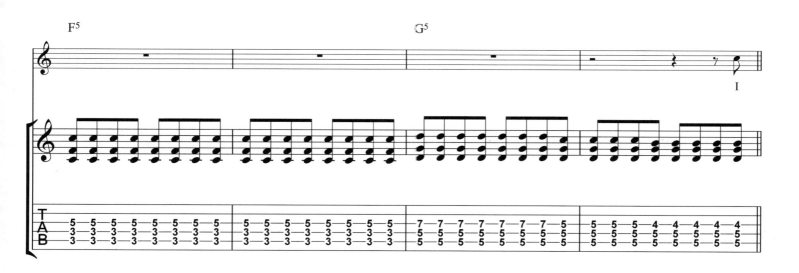

45

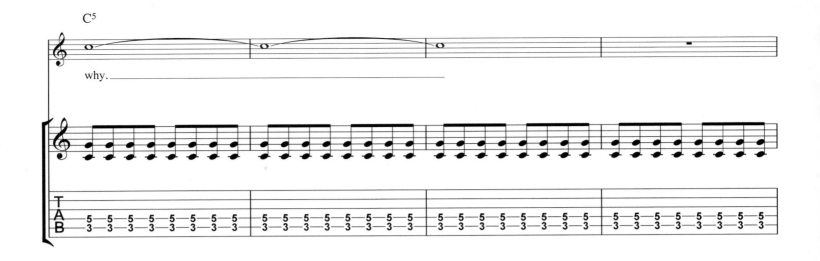

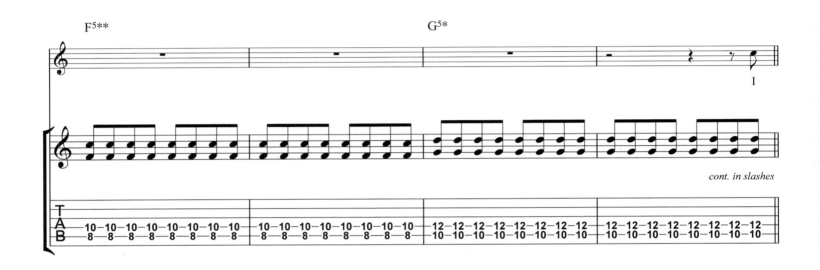

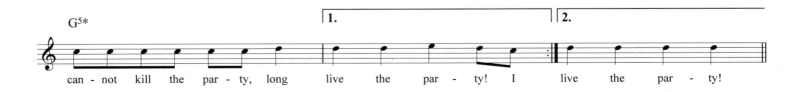

The con - quest will sur -

- vive.

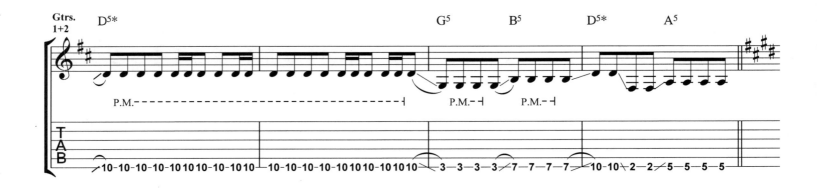

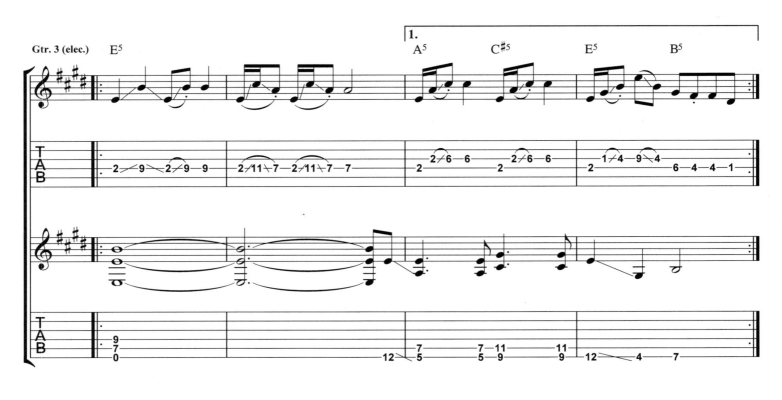

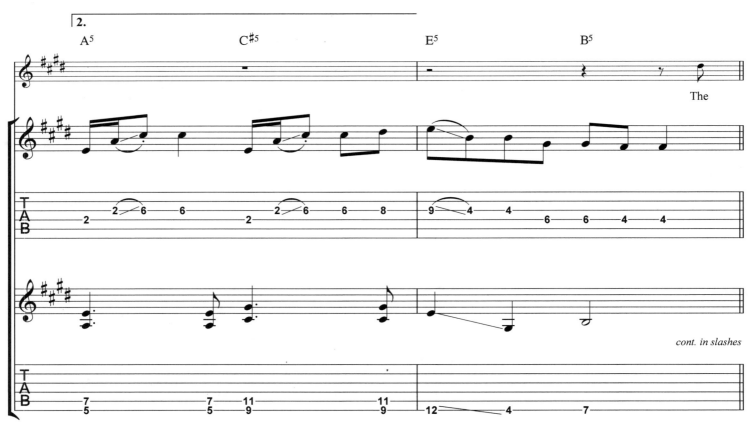

cont. in slashes

50

Bridge

more that you can give it, then the more it will be, ___ and if you do not have it, you can

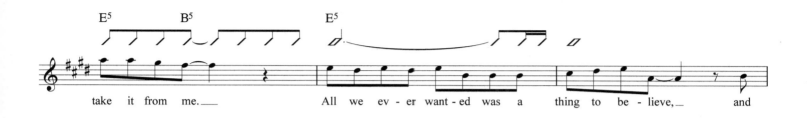

take it from me. ___ All we ev-er want-ed was a thing to be-lieve, ___ and

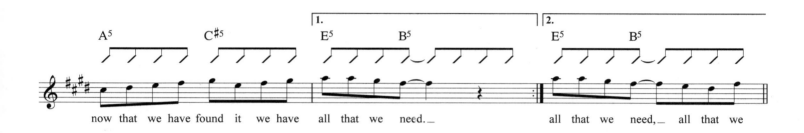

now that we have found it we have all that we need. ___ all that we need, ___ all that we

Outro

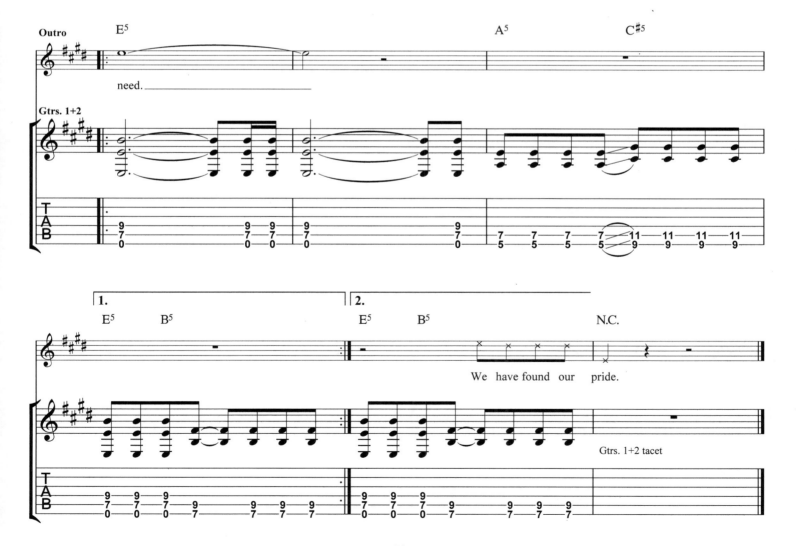

need. ___

Gtrs. 1+2

We have found our pride.

Gtrs. 1+2 tacet

PARTY HARD

Words & Music by Andrew Wilkes-Krier

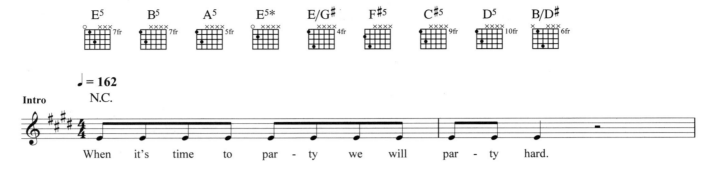

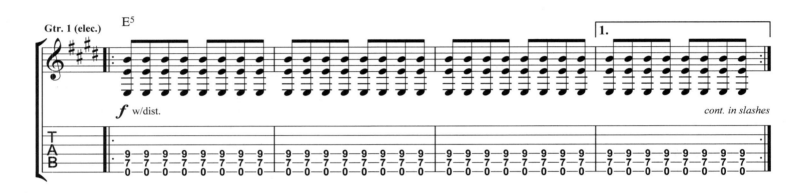

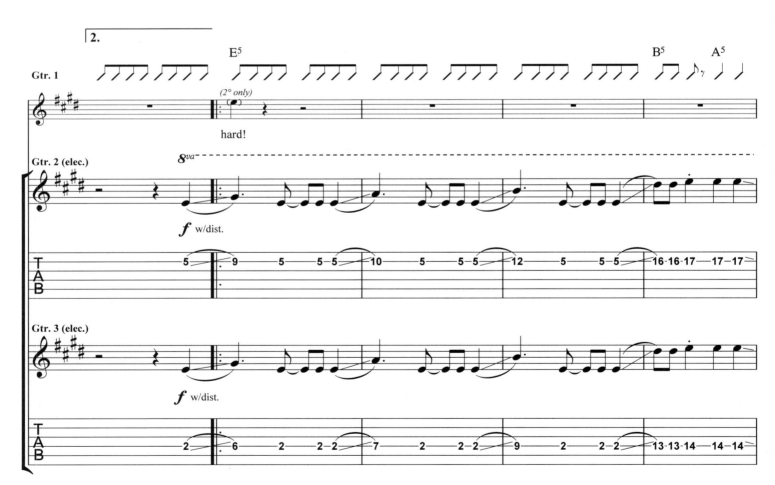

PARTY TIL YOU PUKE

Words & Music by Andrew Wilkes-Krier

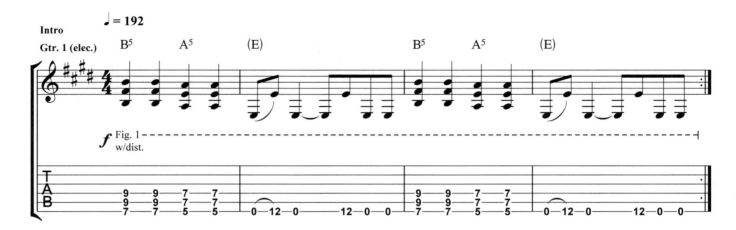

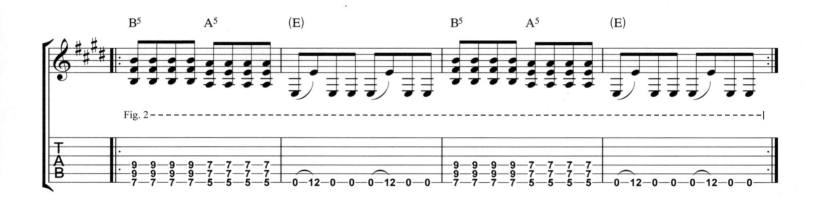

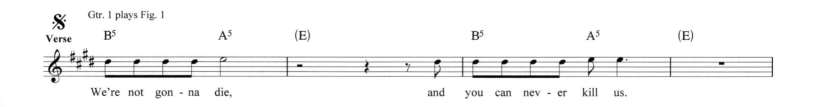

We're not gon - na die, and you can nev - er kill us.

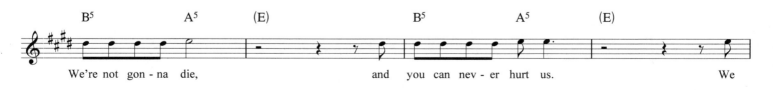

We're not gon - na die, and you can nev - er hurt us. We

NEVER LET DOWN

Words & Music by Andrew Wilkes-Krier

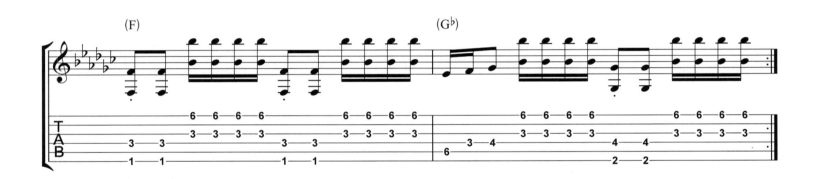

61

SHE IS BEAUTIFUL

Words & Music by Andrew Wilkes-Krier

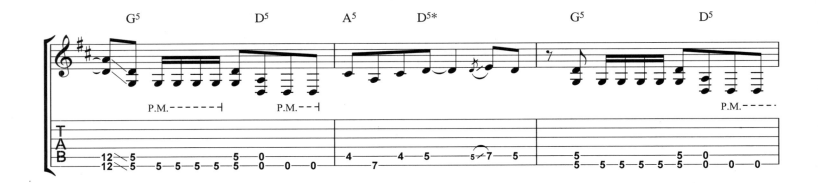

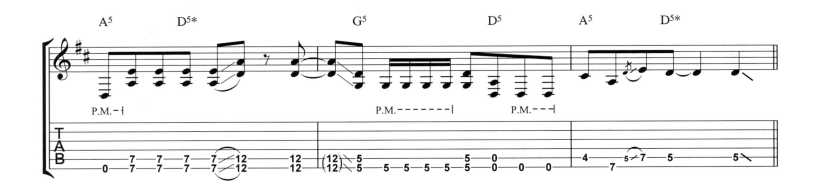

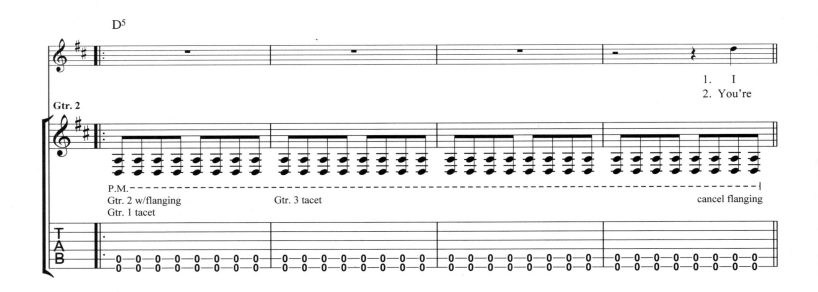

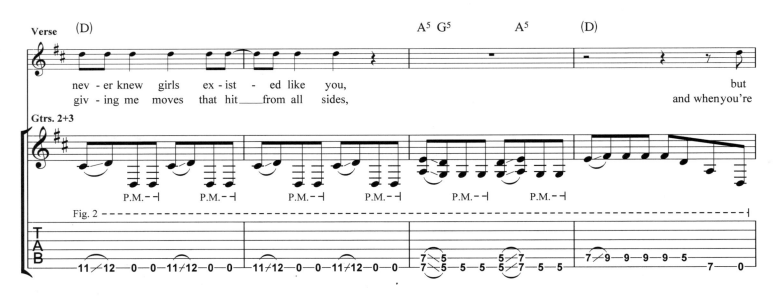

68

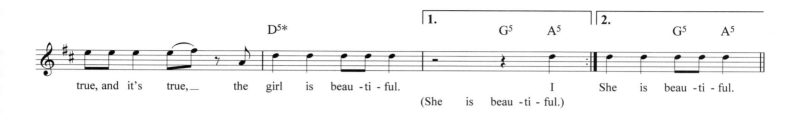

throw it a - way___ and talk to you.___
liv - ing one time, and I want you.___ } She looks good, she looks good, and it's

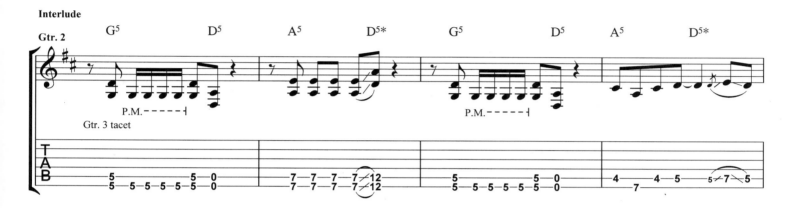

1.   G5   A5   **2.**   G5   A5

true, and it's true,___ the girl is beau - ti - ful.   I   She is beau - ti - ful.
(She is beau - ti - ful.)

Interlude

Gtr. 2

G5   D5   A5   D5*   G5   D5   A5   D5*

P.M.----┤   P.M.-----┤

Gtr. 3 tacet

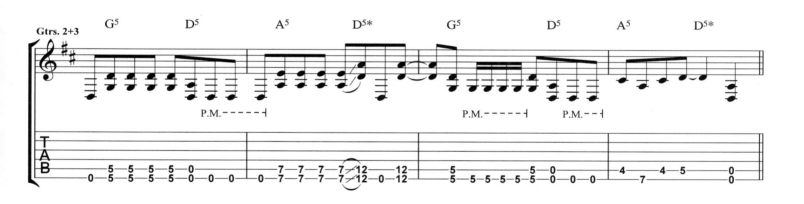

Gtrs. 2+3

G5   D5   A5   D5*   G5   D5   A5   D5*

P.M.-----┤   P.M.-----┤   P.M.--┤

Chorus   (D)   A5   G5

She is beau - ti - ful,   she is beau - ti - ful,   na,   na,___ na,   na,

NOT GOING TO BED

Words & Music by Andrew Wilkes-Krier

Gtr. 2 plays Fig. 2

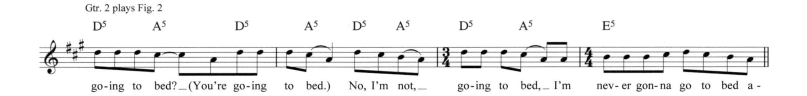

go-ing to bed?_(You're go-ing to bed.) No, I'm not,_ go-ing to bed,_ I'm nev-er gon-na go to bed a-

Verse

Gtr. 2

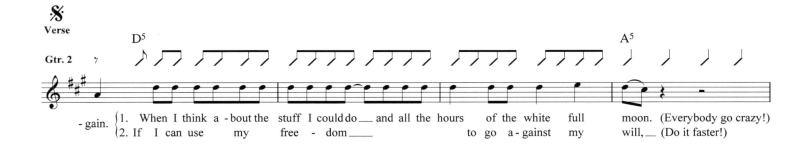

-gain. 1. When I think a-bout the stuff I could do_ and all the hours of the white full moon. (Everybody go crazy!)
2. If I can use my free-dom_____ to go a-gainst my will,_ (Do it faster!)

I get ex-cit-ed when the num-ber is late,_ but I get an-gry when it ends so soon._ (I want you to dance!) Tell_
then I will use my free-dom, and you can bet I will.___ (Real-ly get it now.)

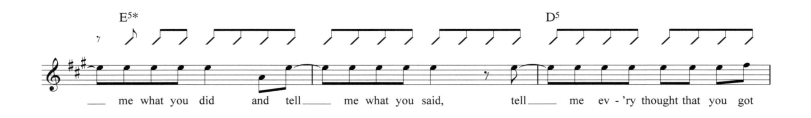

___ me what you did and tell___ me what you said, tell___ me ev-'ry thought that you got

up in your head._____ (I said,) "I'll go to sleep when I'm old or I'm_ dead." I'm not

Gtr. 2 plays Fig. 2

Chorus

go-ing to bed,_ (You're go-ing to bed.) I'm not go-ing to bed._ Who's
(I'm nev-er gon-na sleep a-gain.)_

go-ing to bed? (You're go-ing to bed.) No, I'm not,_ I won't,_ I won't, I won't ev-er go to bed a-

72

73

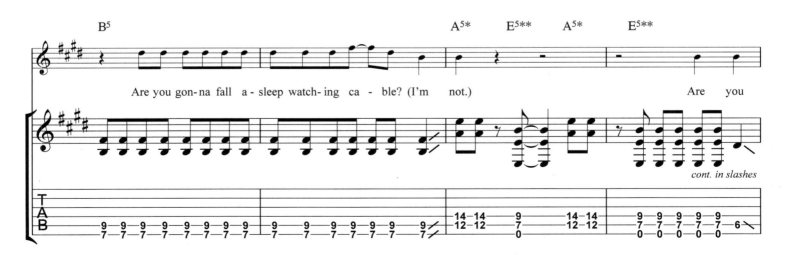

gon - na let your bo - dy do a num - ber on you___ and give you shiv - ers till you can't stand

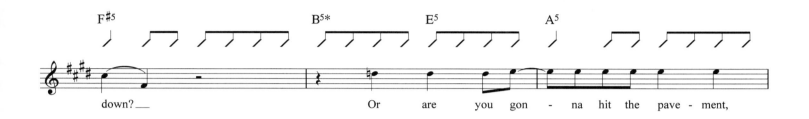

down?___ Or are you gon - na hit the pave - ment,

smok - ing ev - 'ry joint in town?_____

Interlude

I'm

not.

I'm not

Gtr. 2 plays Fig. 2

Chorus

D⁵ A⁵ D⁵ A⁵ D⁵ A⁵ D⁵ A⁵

go - ing to bed,___ (You're go - ing to bed.) I'm not go - ing to bed.___
(I'm

E⁵ D⁵ A⁵ D⁵ A⁵ D⁵ A⁵

Who's go - ing to bed? (You're go - ing to bed.)___ No, I'm not!___
nev - er gon - na sleep a - gain.)___

D⁵ A⁵ E⁵

I won't,___ I won't, I won't ev - er go to bed a -

Gtr. 2

Outro

D⁵ A⁵ D⁵ A⁵ D⁵ A⁵ D⁵ A⁵ D⁵ A⁵ D⁵ A⁵

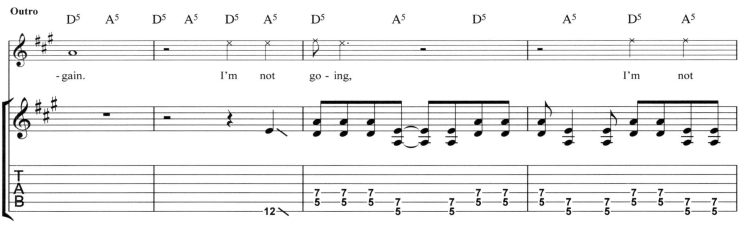

- gain. I'm not go - ing, I'm not

D⁵ A⁵ D⁵ A⁵ D⁵ A⁵ D⁵

go - ing to bed,___ (go - ing to bed,) I'm not go ing to bed a - gain.___

TOTALLY STUPID

Words & Music by Andrew Wilkes-Krier

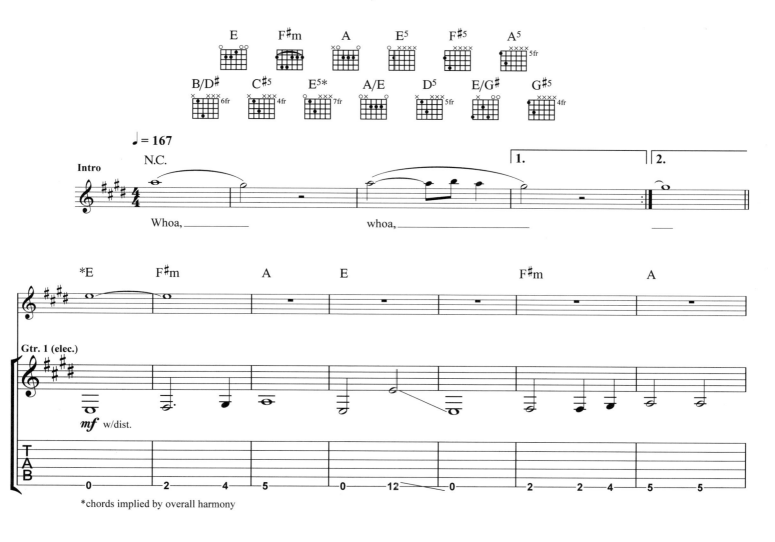

*chords implied by overall harmony

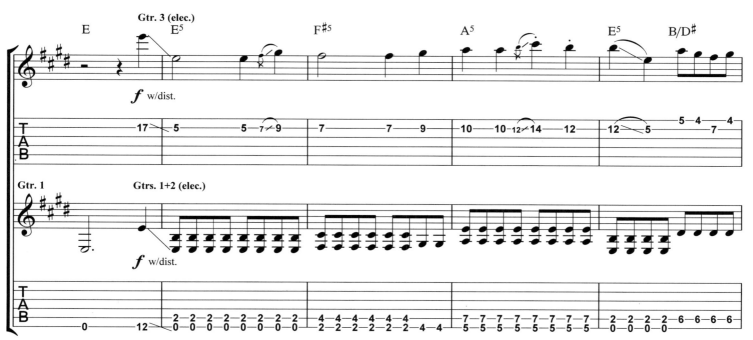

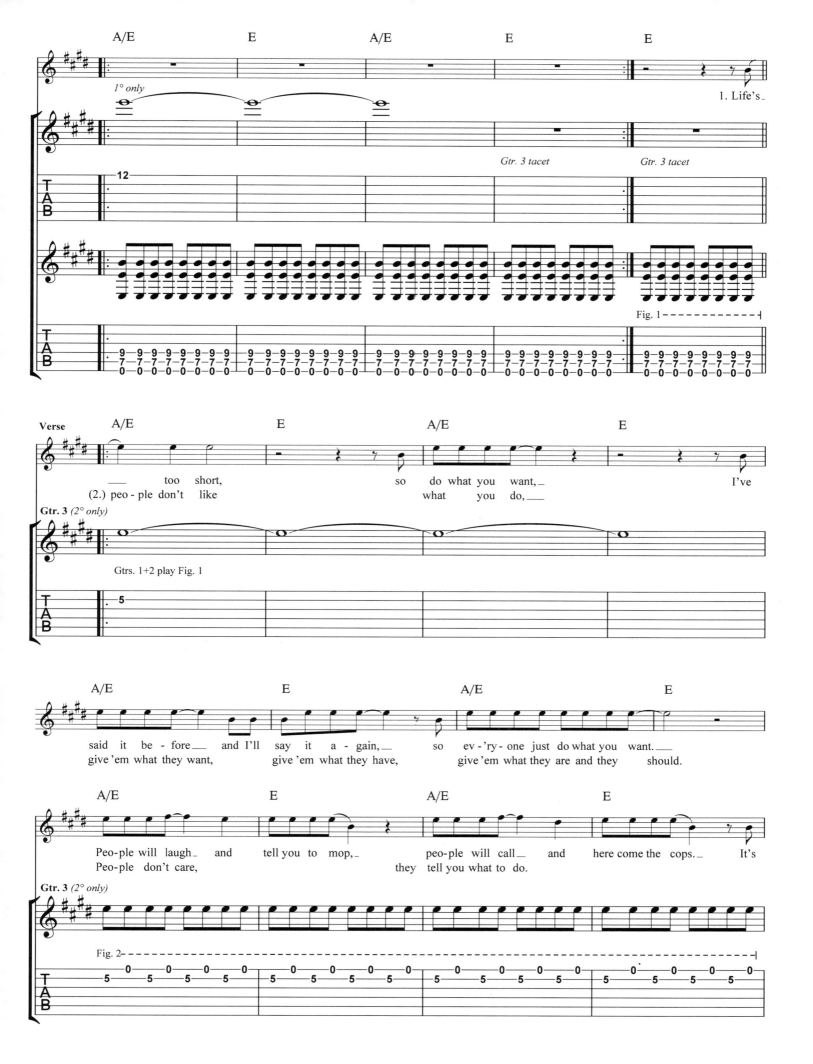

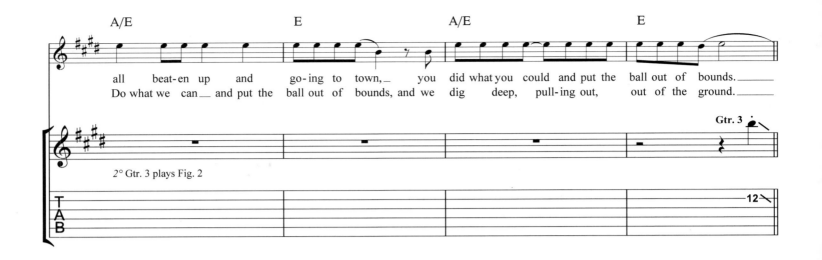

all beat-en up and go-ing to town,___ you did what you could and put the ball out of bounds._____
Do what we can___ and put the ball out of bounds, and we dig deep, pull-ing out, out of the ground._____

2° Gtr. 3 plays Fig. 2

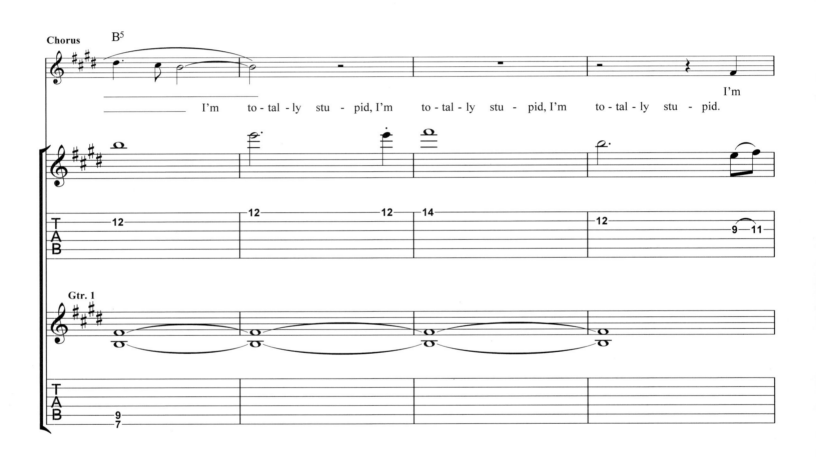

Chorus

I'm to - tal - ly stu - pid, I'm to - tal - ly stu - pid, I'm to - tal - ly stu - pid. I'm

Gtr. 1

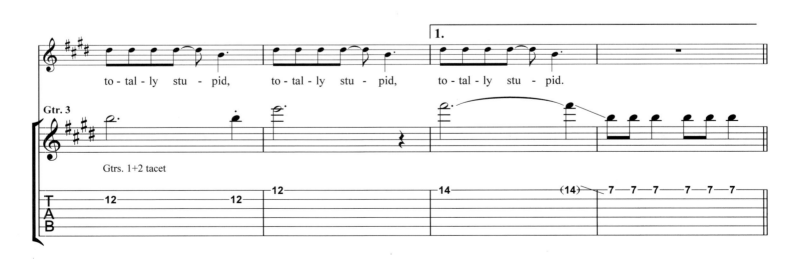

to - tal - ly stu - pid, to - tal - ly stu - pid, to - tal - ly stu - pid.

Gtrs. 1+2 tacet

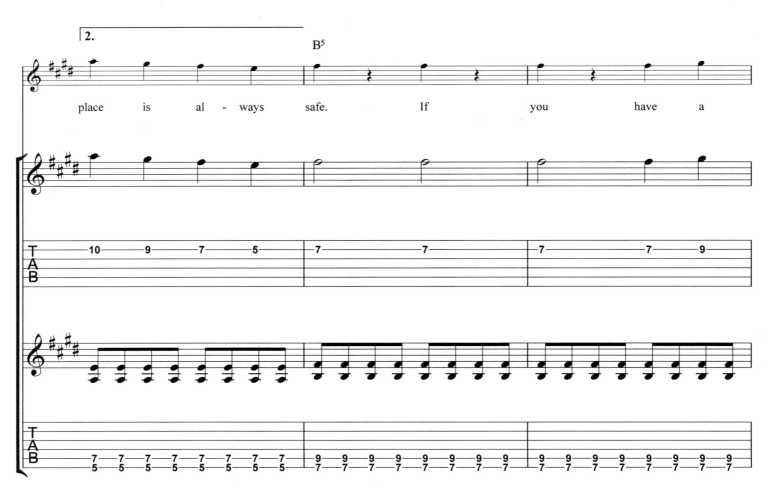

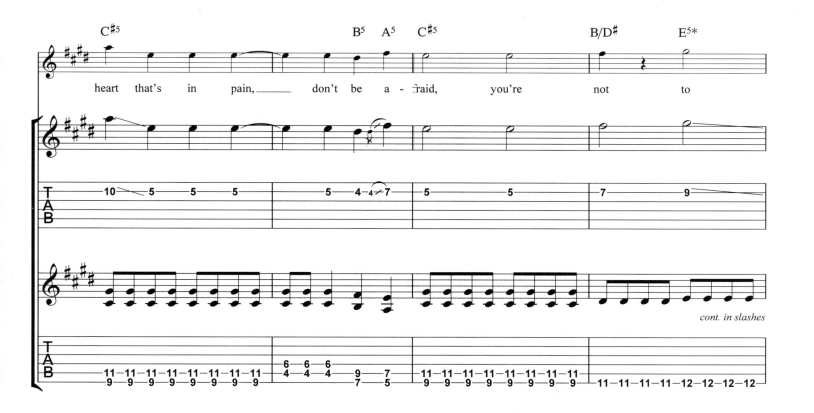

heart that's in pain,_____ don't be a - fraid, you're not to

blame.   There's   a   bet - ter world in - side of us,

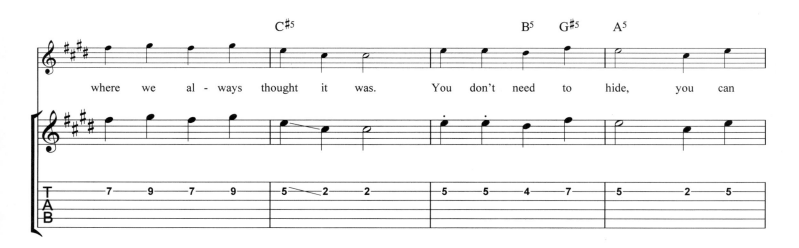

where we al - ways thought it was.   You don't need to hide, you can

op - en up your eyes and you'll dis - cov - - er that there is an -

Free time

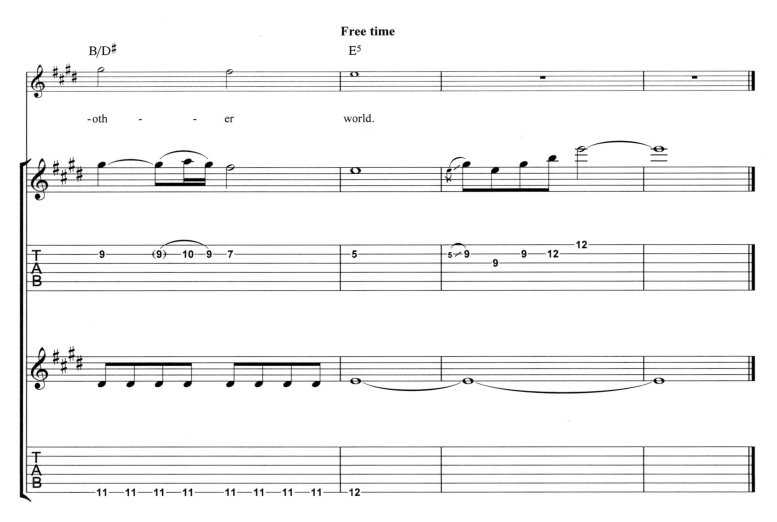

-oth - - er world.

FUN NIGHT

Words & Music by Andrew Wilkes-Krier

READY TO DIE

Words & Music by Andrew Wilkes-Krier

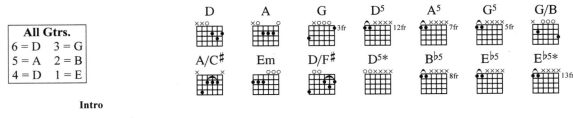

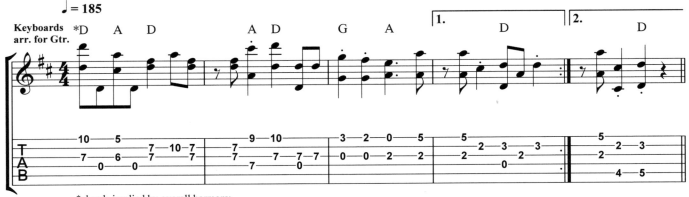

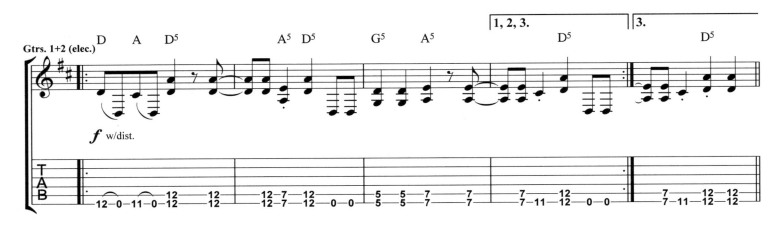

*chords implied by overall harmony

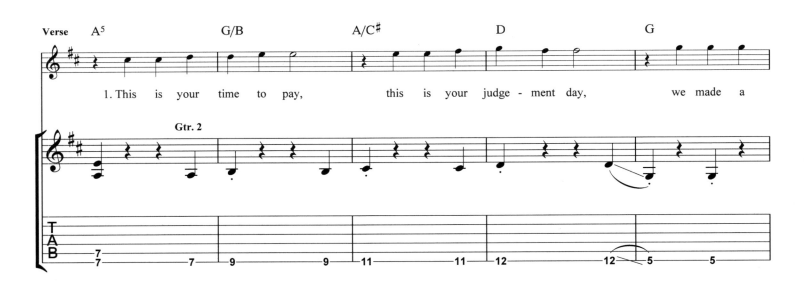

Chorus

91

better get rea-dy to die.

(Get rea-dy to die.)

2. Your life is ov-er now, your life is run-ning out. When your time is at an end,

then it's time to kill a-gain. We cut with-out a knife, we live in

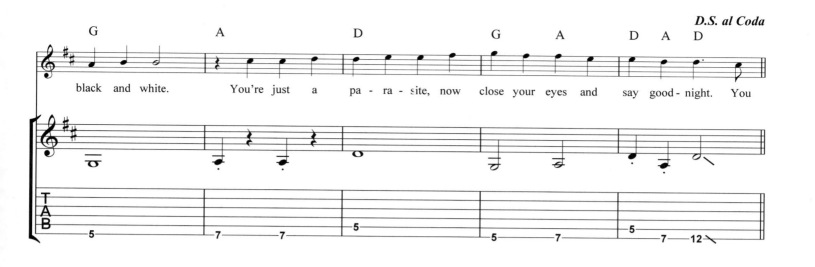

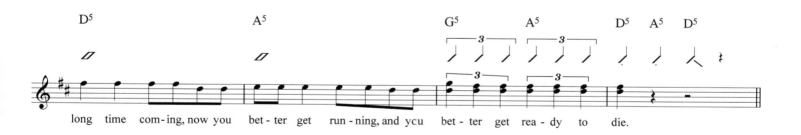

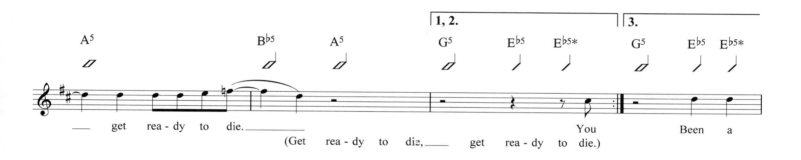

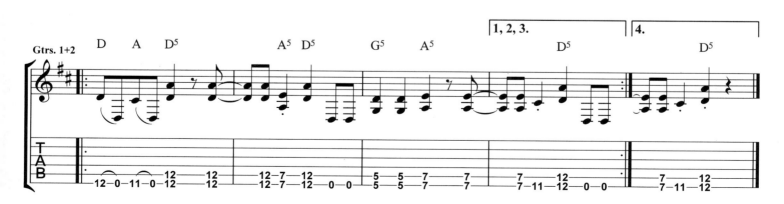

THE MOVING ROOM

Words & Music by Andrew Wilkes-Krier

Bridge

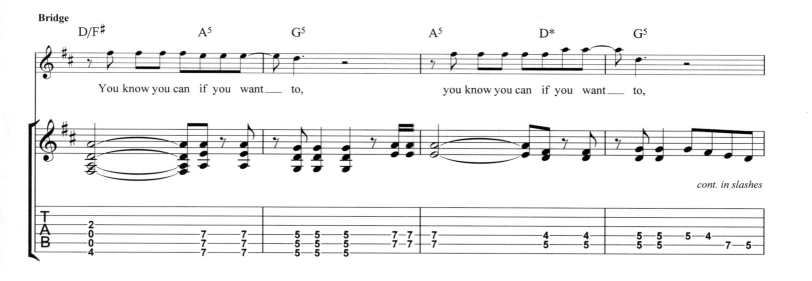

You know you can if you want to, you know you can if you want to,

cont. in slashes

you know you can if you want to, if you want to, if you want to, wel-come to the mov-ing

Chorus

Gtr. 1 plays Fig. 1

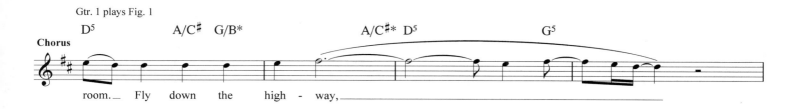

room. Fly down the high - way,

in - to a dream - land, whoa.

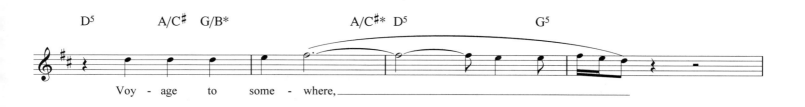

Voy - age to some - where,

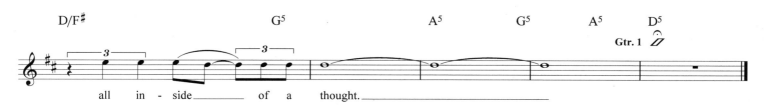

all in - side of a thought.

I LOVE NYC

Words & Music by Andrew Wilkes-Krier

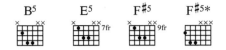

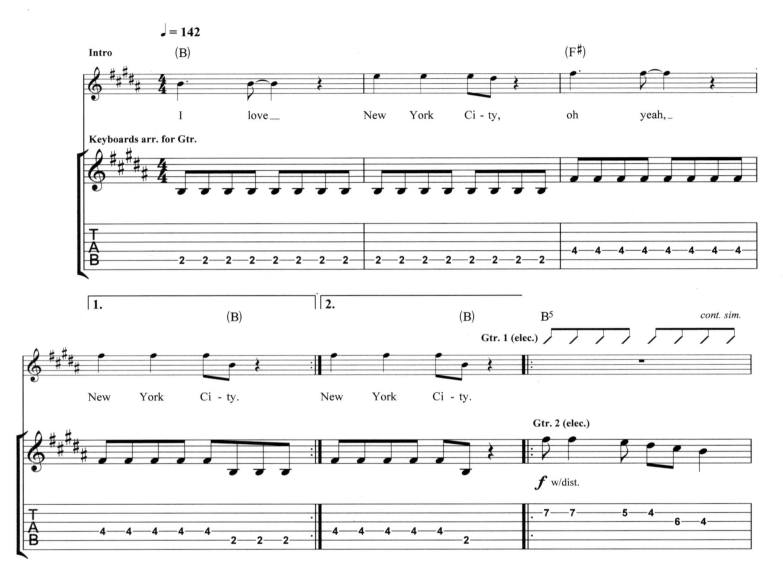

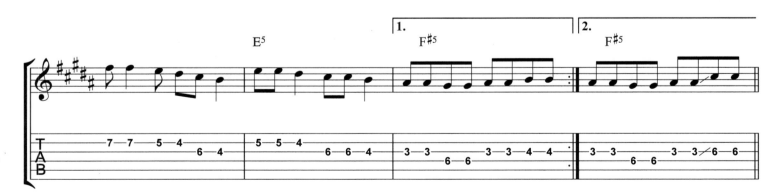

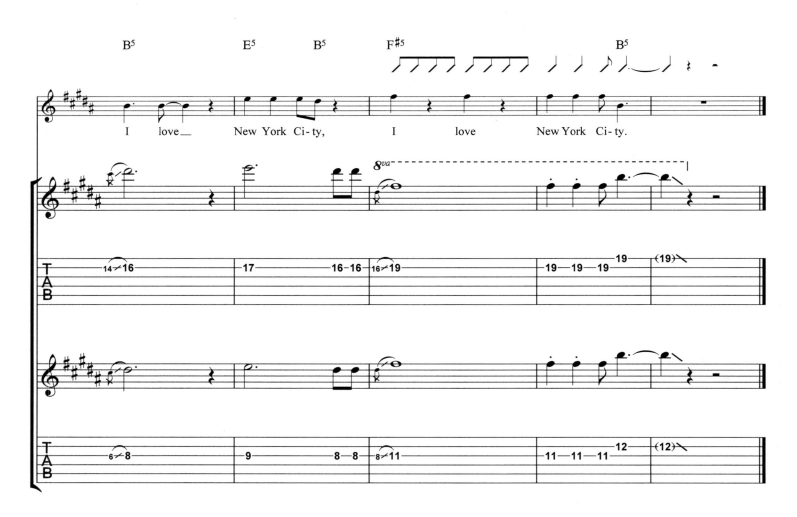

I GET WET

Words & Music by Andrew Wilkes-Krier

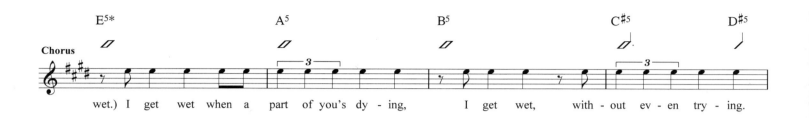

really don't care, I really don't care, you're never gonna go nowhere. (I get

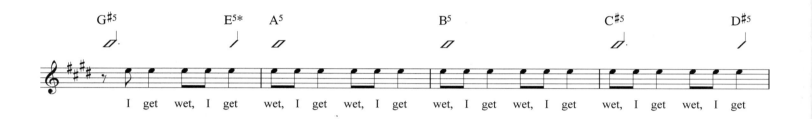

Chorus

wet.) I get wet when a part of you's dying, I get wet, without even trying.

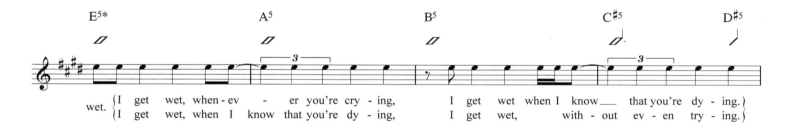

I get wet, I get wet, I get wet, I get wet, I get wet, I get wet, I get wet, I get

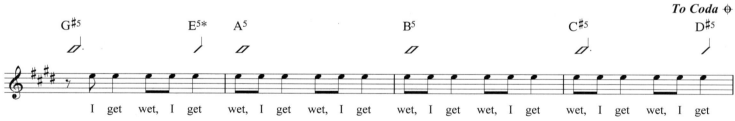

wet. {I get wet, whenever you're crying, I get wet when I know that you're dying. / I get wet, when I know that you're dying, I get wet, without even trying.}

To Coda

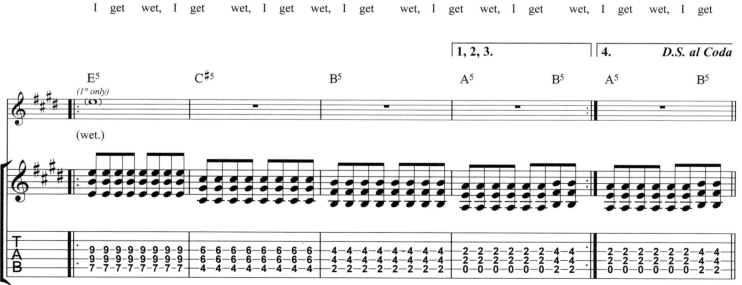

1, 2, 3.   *4.*   *D.S. al Coda*

I get wet, I get wet, I get wet, I get wet, I get wet, I get wet, I get wet, I get

(wet.)

WE PARTY (YOU SHOUT)

Words & Music by Andrew Wilkes-Krier

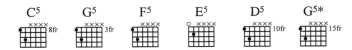

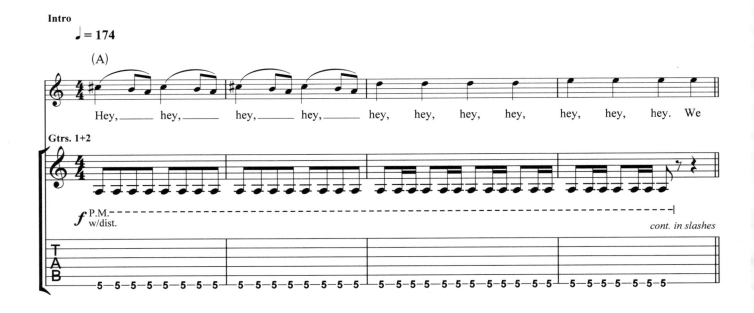

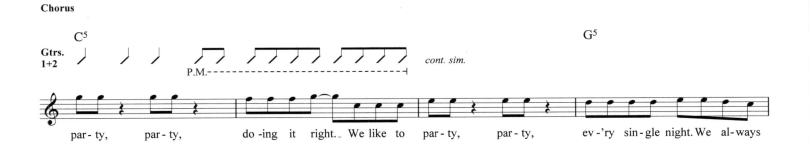

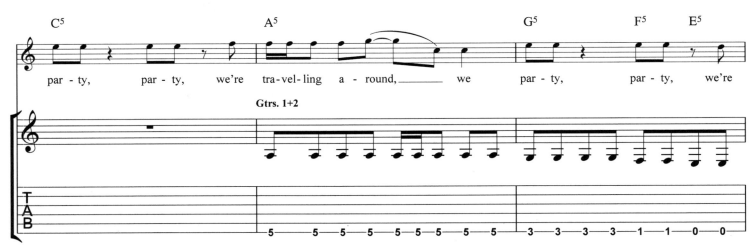

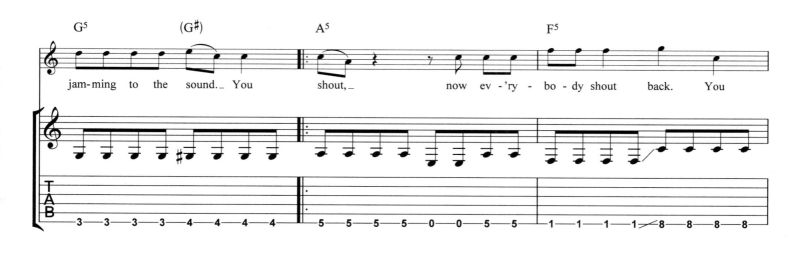

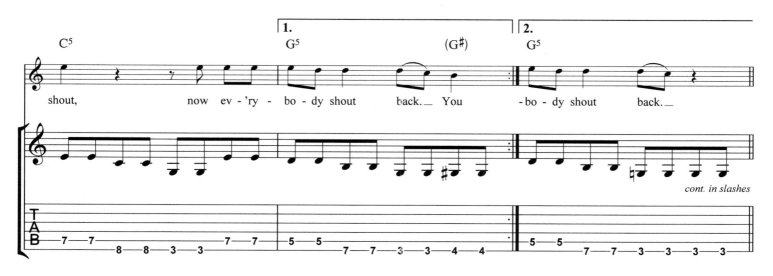

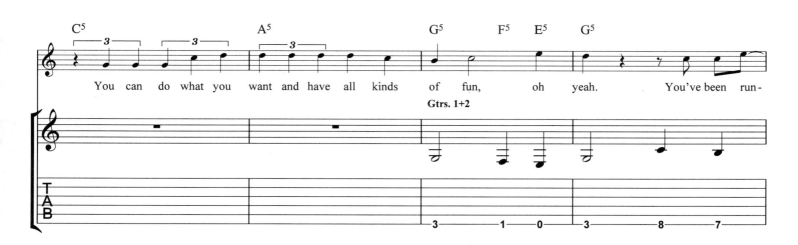

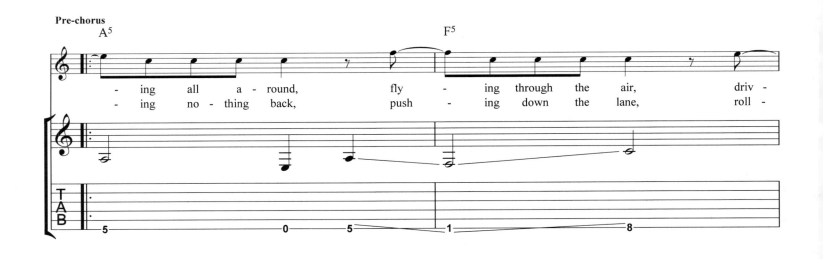

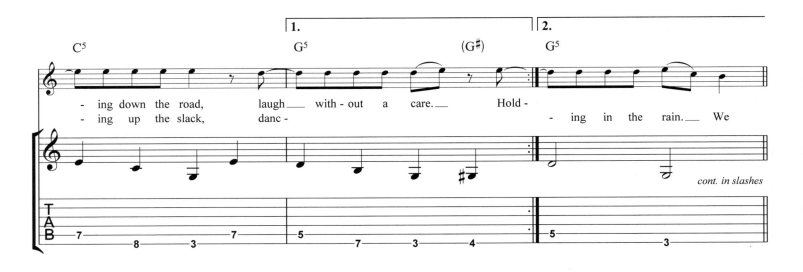

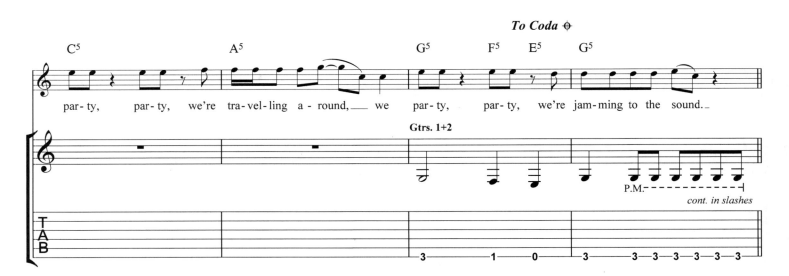

108

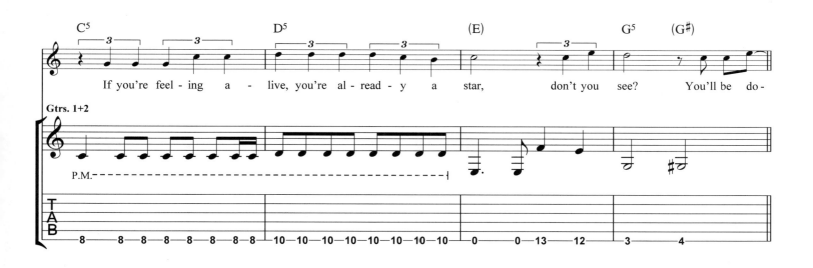

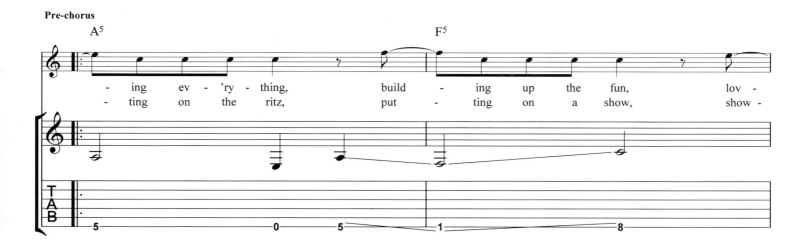

ANDREW W.K.